Linking art to the world around us

artyfacts

Minibeasts

Abbey
Children's
Books

CONCEPT

Publisher: Felicia Law

Design: Tracy Carrington

Editorial Planning: Karen Foster

Research and Development: Gerry Bailey, Alec Edgington

PROJECT DEVELOPMENT

Project Director: Karen Foster

Editors: Claire Sipi, Hazel Songhurst, Samantha Sweeney

Design Director: Tracy Carrington

Design Manager: Flora Awolaja

Design and DTP: Claire Penny, Paul Montague, James Thompson, Mark Dempsey

Photo and Art Editor: Andrea Sadler

Illustrator: Jan Smith

Model Artist: Sophie Dean

Further models: Sue Partington, Abigail Dean

Digital Workflow: Edward MacDermott

Production: Victoria Grimsell, Christina Brown

Scanning: Acumen Colour Ltd

Published by Abbey Children's Books
(a division of Abbey Home Media Group)

Abbey Home Media Group
435-437 Edgware Road
London W2 1TH
United Kingdom

© 2002 Abbey Home Media Group plc

All rights reserved. No part of this publication may be reproduced, stored in a retrieval system, or transmitted, in any form or by any means, electronic, mechanical, photocopying, recording or otherwise, without prior written permission from the publisher.

Printed and bound by L-Rex Printing Co. Ltd, Hong Kong

FRONT COVER IMAGES: RICHARD SHIELL/ OXFORD SCIENTIFIC FILMS; CNRI/ SCIENCE PHOTO LIBRARY; DAVID DENNIS/ OXFORD SCIENTIFIC FILMS; NIGEL CATTLIN/ HOLT STUDIOS

Linking art to the world around us

artyfacts
Minibeasts

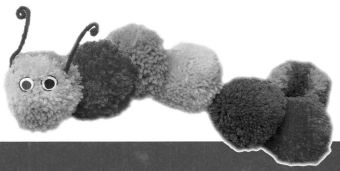

Contents

WRITTEN BY Steve Parker and Polly Goodman

Polka dots

Ladybirds are small beetles with a round bright red or black body covered with black, white or red spots. There are over 3,400 different species, or kinds, of ladybird living all over the world. Farmers and gardeners welcome them because they are helpful insects. Ladybirds feed on aphids and insects which damage crops by sucking out their sap. One tiny ladybird can eat up to 100 aphids a day!

A LONG SLEEP

To stay alive during the cold winter months, ladybirds hibernate, or sleep, until the spring. Every autumn, large groups of ladybirds gather together close to where they will hibernate. These places are usually where the ladybirds will be sheltered from the weather – under stones or tree roots. Some species collect in such large numbers that they can cause ladybird plagues! The average number of two-spotted ladybirds in a group, for example, is about a thousand.

SPOT COUNT

There are two-spotted, seven-spotted, nine-spotted, ten-spotted and even thirteen-spotted ladybirds. The spots may look like decoration, but they have an important purpose. Together with the ladybird's bright-red wings, the spot pattern warns hungry predators that the ladybird will taste horrible! This is because ladybirds ooze nasty-tasting yellow blood from their knee-joints. So, once a bird has eaten one kind of ladybird, it will never touch another like it again!

Minibeasts

Ladybird racetrack

WHAT YOU NEED

ruler

card

glue

tissue paper

scissors

sequins

paint and brush

pencil

gold paper

5 small empty matchboxes

1 Cut out a variety of leaf shapes from tissue paper and flower shapes from the gold paper.

2 Stick 5 leaf pattern lanes on card. Number each leaf.

4 Stick your boxes on the card at the finishing line of the game.

5 Draw and cut out a shape like this. Fold along the dotted lines.

3 Paint 5 matchboxes different colours.

6 Fold up and glue the shape to make a dice. Stick on sequins for the dots. From the card, make 5 ladybird counters for each matchbox.

Play this game with two or more friends!

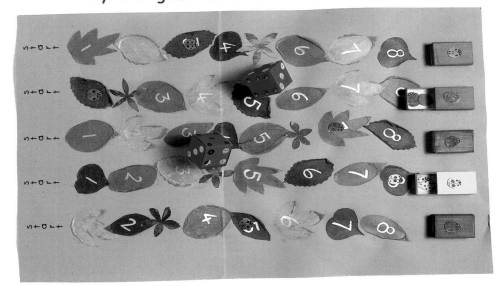

To play: Choose a lane, and throw a 6 to start a counter. If you land on a flower, the counter goes back to the beginning. The winner is the first player to get all five ladybird counters in their matchbox.

Honeycombs

WAX NESTS

The wax nests are called honeycombs. There are about 20,000 different kinds of bees in the world, but only the honey bee makes enough honey and wax for people to use.

BUSY COLONIES

Honey bees live and work together in large groups, called colonies. Each colony has one queen bee and thousands of female worker bees. There are also hundreds of male bees, called drones. Each bee has a special job. The queen bee's only job is to lay eggs. The male drones mate with the queen. The worker bees collect food and build the honeycomb.

Honey bees depositing nectar and pollen in the honeycomb.

BUILDING THE HONEYCOMB

The honeycomb is often built inside the hollow of a tree. It is made up of many six-sided, or hexagonal, cells. The worker bees produce the wax from special glands on their body. The cells are used for the eggs and larvae, and to store pollen and honey.

SPECIAL FOOD

Worker bees collect pollen and also suck liquid nectar from flowers, which they store in their stomachs. They put the nectar and pollen in the honeycomb, where the nectar turns into honey. The honey feeds the workers and the young bees growing in the comb. For their first three days, young bees are also fed a special food called royal jelly. This is the only food fed to young queen bees.

Bees are furry, flying insects which feed on flowering plants. They live everywhere in the world except near the North and South poles. They make honey to feed themselves and their young, and wax to build their nests.

Minibeasts

Honey bee home

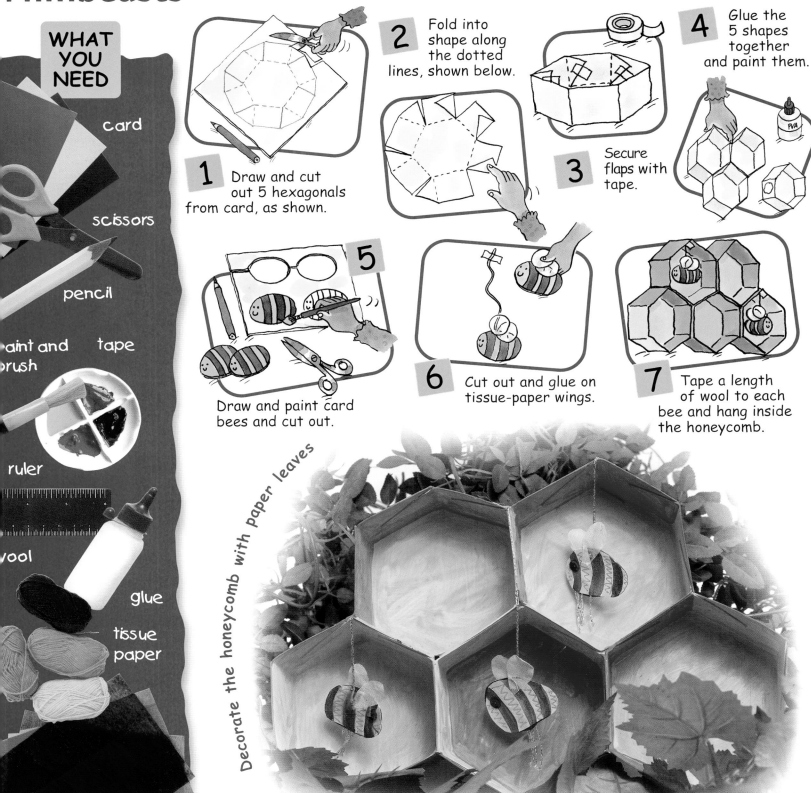

WHAT YOU NEED

card

scissors

pencil

paint and brush

ruler

wool

glue

tissue paper

1 Draw and cut out 5 hexagonals from card, as shown.

2 Fold into shape along the dotted lines, shown below.

3 Secure flaps with tape.

4 Glue the 5 shapes together and paint them.

5 Draw and paint card bees and cut out.

6 Cut out and glue on tissue-paper wings.

7 Tape a length of wool to each bee and hang inside the honeycomb.

Decorate the honeycomb with paper leaves

Glass wings

Dragonflies are beautiful, fast-flying insects with a colourful, slender body and four lacy wings. They have large compound eyes, made up of lots of tiny lenses, which help them spot their prey up to six metres away. Dragonflies live close to rivers, lakes and ponds, where they hover and dart through the air, catching smaller insects for food.

GROWING UP

Dragonflies grow up in three stages, changing from an egg to a nymph, and then to a fully grown adult. The female lays her eggs in shallow water, or on a water plant.

After one or two weeks, the egg hatches into a nymph, which looks more like a fish than an insect. It has no wings and breathes through gills. It eats insects and small water animals. The nymph lives underwater for one to five years. As it slowly grows, it sheds its skin, or moults, about twelve times. When it finally leaves the water, the nymph moults one last time. It is now a magnificent, fully-grown dragonfly.

SPEEDY WINGS

The dragonfly's large wings and thin body make it the fastest-flying insect. It can reach speeds of 90 kilometres an hour, which helps it to catch prey, but also to escape from enemies, such as birds. Dragonflies beat their shimmering, gauzy wings up and down one pair at a time, up to a hundred times a second. A dragonfly's body can be green, red or blue with black, yellow or white patterns on it.

Dragonfly fan

WHAT YOU NEED

card

glue

netting

pencil

sequins

paint and brush

scissors

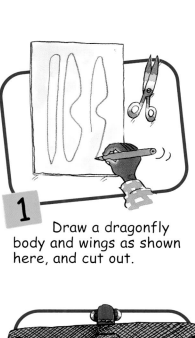

1 Draw a dragonfly body and wings as shown here, and cut out.

2 Cover the wings with net material and paint.

3 Paint the body and decorate with glittery sequins. Glue on large sequins for the eyes.

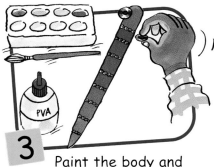

4 Glue the wings onto the body.

You could fix your dazzling dragonfly to the wall or a window

Caterpillars

Caterpillars are the second stage in the life of a butterfly. When a butterfly egg hatches, the tiny worm-like larva or caterpillar crawls out and begins to eat.

TIGHT FIT

As the caterpillar eats, it grows bigger. But unlike most animals, its skin does not grow with it. Before long, the caterpillar's skin becomes too tight, and it has to shed it. A split appears in the skin, near the caterpillar's head. The caterpillar then wriggles out of the old, tight skin. This shedding usually happens several times in a caterpillar's life. In regions which are neither too hot nor too cold, the caterpillar stage lasts for two to four weeks.

But in cold climates, it can take two or three years to change from caterpillar to butterfly.

RINGS ON LEGS

A caterpillar's body has 13 rings, or segments, as well as a head. A pair of legs is attached to each of the first three segments. Each leg has five joints. On the abdomen, inside which food is digested, there are four or five pairs of softer legs, called prolegs. The head has six simple eyes on each side, and a pair of pointed feelers or antennae with which the caterpillar guides itself along. To scare off predators, some caterpillars may be covered in hairs, bristles or spines. Others have false eye-spots or can squirt an unpleasant fluid.

Crawling caterpillar

WHAT YOU NEED

card

pencil

scissors

glue

pipe cleaners

wool

1 Draw and cut out two card rings, with smaller circles cut out inside them.

2 Wind wool around both card rings until the hole in the middle has disappeared.

3 Cut through the wool between the two cards.

4 Tie a piece of wool between the rings and knot it. Leave a length of wool at both ends to attach to the next pompom.

5 Make five more coloured pompoms. Cut out two small card circles for the eyes and glue them to the front pompom.

Make a friendly, fluffy caterpillar to crawl across your floor

Glue on curled pipe cleaners to make the caterpillar's antennae.

11

Snail shells

Snails are a kind of mollusc, an animal which has a soft body usually protected by a hard shell. Snails are related to slugs There are about 77,000 different kinds of snails and slugs.

HOMES THAT GROW

Snails have a single spiral shell. When a snail is threatened, it can pull the soft part of its body inside the hard shell for protection. Other animals, such as crabs, have rigid, or fixed, shells which have to be replaced as they grow. But a snail's shell is part of its body and grows with the soft part.

DAMP AND DRY SPELLS

As a snail moves it produces a sticky slime to help it slide across the ground. It moves its muscular 'foot' in a wave-like movement to propel itself forward on the slime.

Snails like dampness. In dry weather, the snail stays inside its shell, sealing itself in with a 'door' of dried slime. The snail stays inside the safety of its home until it rains again.

SHELLY LID

Not all snails live on the land: many, such as pond snails, live in water. Snails that live in the sea are called marine snails. Many kinds of marine snails have a 'lid', called an operculum, which seals off the snail whenever it draws itself inside its shell. The operculum stops predators from attacking and eating the snail. Marine snails often have very colourful or patterned shells. You can sometimes find these shells washed up on beaches.

Minibeasts

Patterned spirals

Make stunning shell spirals with bright paints and patterns

WHAT YOU NEED

bowl

wooden spoon

cooking oil

baking tray

flour

paints

paintbrush

glue

glitter

1 In a bowl, mix flour, water and cooking oil into a dough. Add more flour if the dough is too sticky. Knead the dough, cover it and put in the fridge for half an hour.

2 Sprinkle some flour on a flat surface and roll the dough into long tubes.

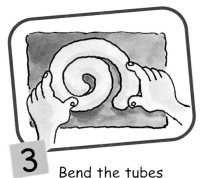

3 Bend the tubes into spirals.

4 Place the spirals on a baking tray and bake them in a hot oven for 30 minutes.

5 When cool, decorate your spirals with paint and glitter.

13

Beautiful butterfly

The butterfly is one of the most beautiful flying insects. It has two pairs of brightly coloured or patterned wings. If you could look at the wings under a microscope, you would see that they are made of lots of tiny, overlapping scales.

BUTTERFLY BIRD

There are between 15,000 and 20,000 different kinds of butterfly in the world. The Queen Alexandra's birdwing has a wingspan as big as a bird's, while the western pygmy blue is smaller than a fingernail.

COLOURED WINGS

Butterflies are painted in all the colours of the rainbow. Some are bright, some are pale and some have amazing patterns. Many have shimmering wings, which change colour when they move, as light reflects between each tiny wing scale.

BLENDING IN

The colour and pattern of a butterfly's wings help it to blend in among the flowers it feeds on, making it harder for enemies to see. It also helps the butterfly attract a mate. Some butterflies have wing patterns that look like bigger animals, to scare off predators. The pearly eye butterfly has brown wings marked with spots, which look like large eyes. The southern dogface has markings like a dog's face.

FIRST FLIGHT

A new adult butterfly's wings are soft and crumpled at first. The veins running through them slowly fill with air, and the wings are held out to dry. To fly, the butterfly uses its flight muscles to beat its wings up and down and lift it up, while the bending, flexible edges help push it forwards.

Minibeasts

Butterfly kite

WHAT YOU NEED

ball of string

paint and brush

paper

pencil

scissors

glitter

tape

2 wooden sticks

glue

sequins

1 Fold a sheet of paper in half. Unfold, then draw half a butterfly shape.

2 Paint the half butterfly in bright, bold colours and patterns.

Decorate your butterfly in fantastic bold bright colours!

3 With the paint still wet, fold the sheet over. Open it up to see the whole symmetrical shape!

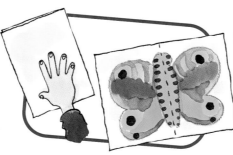

4 When dry, glue onto a second sheet and cut out.

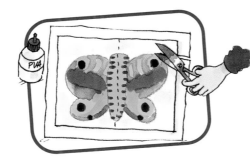

6 Stick on sequins and glitter for decoration. Fly your kite on a windy day.

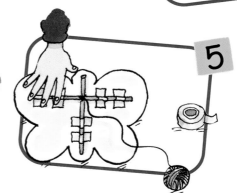

5 Tie the sticks in a cross, leaving a long length of string. Glue to the back of the butterfly.

Fly's eyes

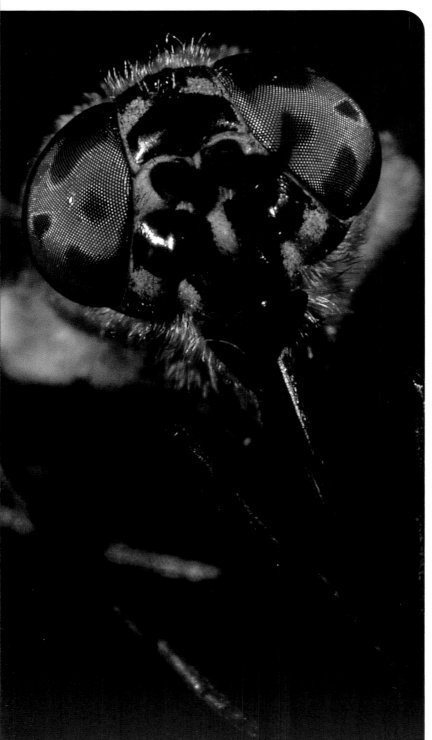

Have you ever tried to catch a housefly? It's usually walking about or standing still. You creep up on it very slowly, or you try a fast grab. But almost every time, the fly is too quick, and buzzes away out of reach. How does it see you coming?

BIG EYES

A fly's eyes look tiny, but they are huge compared to its size. If the fly was as big as you, its eyes would be the size of footballs! They bulge from its head, so it can see almost all around, even behind its back.

TV VISION

A television picture is made up of thousands of tiny dots or bars. From a distance, these merge together into one single scene. A fly sees the world like this, as thousands of tiny dots of light. This is because each fly's eye is not a single part but lots of tiny parts, called facets. The facets face outwards, making the whole eye look like a bunch of pinheads. Each facet picks up, or detects, the light from one small part of a whole view.

ON THE MOVE

Flies do not see in such detail as we do, or see as many different colours. But the smallest movement changes the dot of light received by one facet, and so the fly always sees you coming!

MORE BUG-EYED BUGS

It is not just flies that have multi-part, or compound, eyes. Beetles, butterflies, bees and other insects have them too, but their eyes vary in size, as does the number of facets they have.

Minibeasts

Goggle-eye fly

WHAT YOU NEED

- wire
- foil
- netting
- plastic ball
- scissors
- tissue paper
- brush
- sequins
- silver paint
- glue
- newspaper
- double-sided tape

1 Scrunch up newspaper into 2 body sections and cover with silver foil.

2 Ask an adult to cut the ball in half. Glue sequins all over each half.

3 Join the halves of the ball with double-sided tape. Cover the join with a strip of paper, painted silver.

4 Glue the body and head sections together. Wrap wire around each section for extra support.

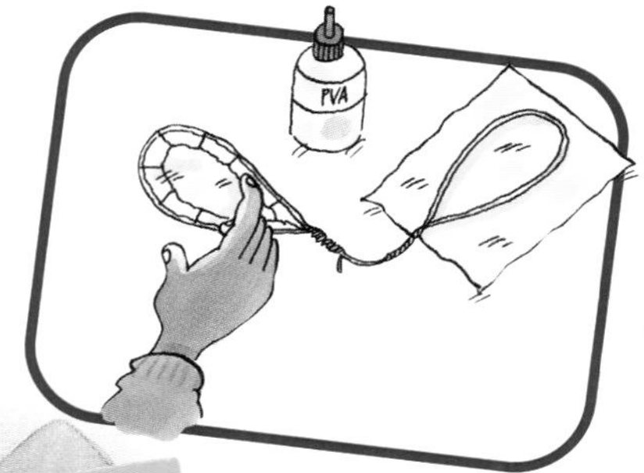

5 Make 2 wire wing frames and cover with white tissue paper.

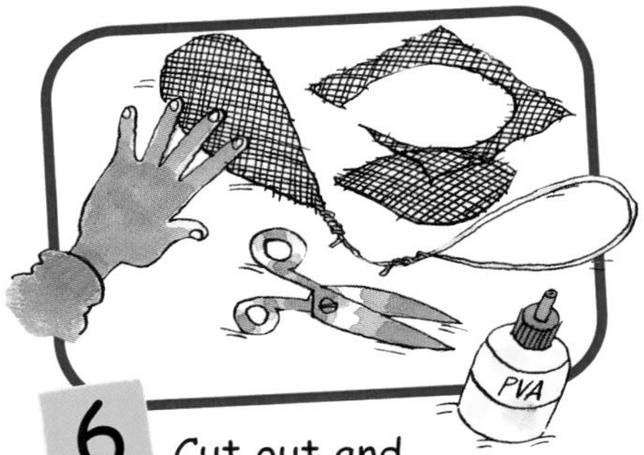

6 Cut out and glue netting across each wing. Attach to the body with wire.

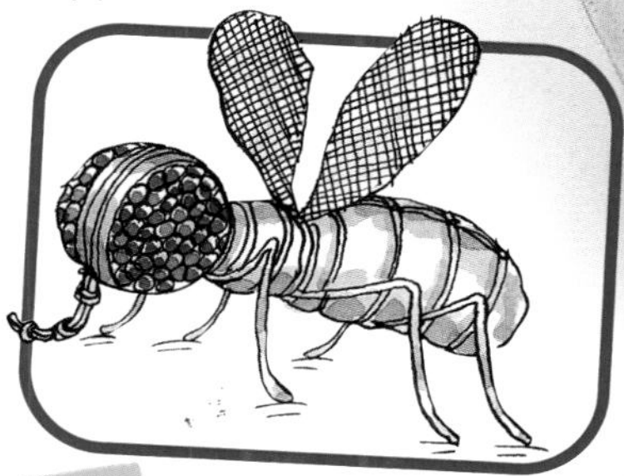

7 Make a mouth-piece from twisted wire. Attach 6 twisted wire legs to the body.

Why not use some strong thread to hang your giant fly from the ceiling?

Lots of legs

Centipedes and millipedes have the most legs of any living creature. The word centipede means 'hundred-footed'. It comes from centi meaning 'one hundred' and pede meaning 'feet'. The word millipede means 'thousand-footed', from milli meaning 'one thousand'. But millipedes do not have thousands of legs – the most they are known to have is 760, in 380 pairs!

JOINTS AND SEGMENTS

The bodies of these worm-like creatures are divided into segments, with jointed legs attached to each segment. Centipedes can have between 15 to 175 pairs of legs. Centipedes have one pair of legs attached to each body segment, but millipedes have two. There are over 2,000 different kinds of centipedes, and over 8,000 different kinds of millipedes in the world. They range from the common garden millipede, just 3 millimetres long, to the giant desert centipede, which can be 30 centimetres long.

POISON JAWS

Centipedes are very different from millipedes. The centipede is a fierce, meat-eating carnivore and also a cannibal! It eats molluscs, worms, and other centipedes. Vegetarian millipedes eat only plants.

The first pair of the centipede's legs have become fangs. They are called poison jaws because they inject the prey with poison which comes from a gland in the centipede's head. Centipedes hunt at night and can run much faster than millipedes.

SELF DEFENCE

Millipedes and centipedes defend themselves against attackers in some surprising ways. The South African millipede squirts foul-smelling chemicals from its skin, while the pill millipede rolls into a ball. And if necessary, all centipedes can afford to shed a few legs – they will soon grow back again!

This bright red centipede looks like a worm with legs!

Minibeasts

Smiley centipede

Make a rainbow-coloured card centipede with dangling dancing legs

WHAT YOU NEED

card

pipe cleaners

ue

sequins

scissors

wool

tape

nut shells

tissue paper

pencil

1 Draw the outline of a centipede and cut out.

2 Fold the centipede body into a concertina.

3 Cut or tear lots of tissue paper strips. Glue them on to create a stripey centipede.

4 Cut lots of lengths of wool for the legs. Tape them to the back of the body so they hang down. Glue nut shells to the ends of the wool for feet.

5 Tape 2 pipe cleaners to the head for antennae. Glue on sequins to give your centipede a smiley face and stick on more for the eyes and button nose.

19

Little pests

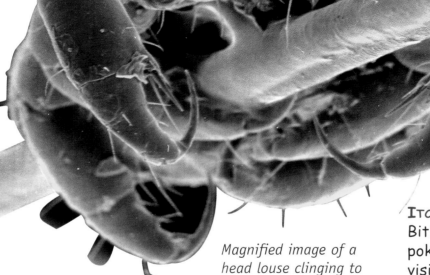

Magnified image of a head louse clinging to a human hair.

Tiny animals called parasites love to drink blood! They stick their needle-sharp mouths through skin and suck up a meal full of goodness. The creatures they bite – including humans – are called their hosts.

FEASTING FLEAS
Fleas are tiny insects, a bit bigger than a pin-head. They live on animals and people, hiding among hairs, fur or feathers. At night they crawl around sucking blood. All animals and birds have their own type of flea. If they can't find their own hosts, cat and dog fleas for example, may take a snack from a person!

NASTY LOUSE
A louse has a flat body and curved claw legs to dig into skin or cling to hair. Most lice are smaller than a grain of rice, and can drink more than five times their own weight in one blood meal! The female louse lays tiny, pale eggs called nits and glues them to hairs or feathers.

ITCHY SPOTS
Biting flies have thin, sharp tube mouths that easily poke through skin. They don't live on a host, but visit for a take-away meal. Gnats and midges are the smallest blood-sucking flies. When a mosquito bites, it pumps special chemicals into the skin so the bite swells into an itchy red spot.

MUNCHING MITES
Minute pests called follicle mites live in our eyelids, in the tiny pits, or follicles, the eyelashes grow from. They feed on skin wax and oil in the follicle and are usually harmless.

SWELLING TICK
Mites are close cousins of spiders, and so are ticks. A tick clings to its host with its beak-like mouth. As it sucks up 20 times its own weight in blood, it swells up to look like a red baked bean. After feeding, the tick drops off its host – full of blood!

Minibeasts

Beastie mobile

Make weird and wonderful minibeasts from a variety of textured materials

WHAT YOU NEED

tissue paper

re

paints and brush

glue

gold thread and needle

1 For a bee, make a body from tissue paper and paint on stripes.

2 Shape wings from wire and glue onto tissue paper.

3 Wrap wings around the body and add little wire legs.

Add scrunched-up tissue paper for the eyes and nose.

4

5 Repeat these stages to create different creatures. Attach all your little pests to gold thread and hang up.

PVA

21

Ants

Imagine being so strong that you could lift up a car. But also imagine having to work all day and all night in a dark, damp and crowded place. This is what ants do. For their size, ants are very strong. They can lift and carry pieces of leaves and twigs many times their own weight. Ants are also the busiest bugs of all. They never take a rest from looking after their nest.

CITY IN A HILL

Some ants live in underground tunnels and some build mounds. Others live inside trees or plants, or make nests from leaves. An underground nest is protected on the outside by a mound of leaves, twigs and soil. Inside is a maze of tunnels and rooms called chambers, where more than a quarter of a million ants live. It is like a huge ant city.

THE ROYAL PALACE

Ants live together in large organized groups called colonies. Each colony has one or more queen ants. Only a queen ant lays eggs. One chamber in the nest is the 'royal palace'. This is the chamber where the queen ant lives. All the other ants are workers, with many different jobs to do.

BABYSITTER ANTS

Some worker ants are like babysitters. When the eggs are laid, they take them away to the 'nursery' chambers in the nest. This is where the eggs hatch into grubs. The babysitter ants feed and look after the young ants until they grow up and become worker ants themselves.

BUSY WORKERS

Other worker ants look after the nest. Some keep the tunnels and chambers clean inside, carrying away litter. Other workers repair any damage and build new tunnels or rooms. Workers travel away from the nest to collect food or to defend it against enemies. The defenders, or soldier ants, are the biggest workers with the largest jaws. A worker ant may have the same job all its life, or change to a different task after a time.

Minibeasts

WHAT YOU NEED

card

pencil

glue

scissors

sequins and star shapes

a box lid

silver paint

marble

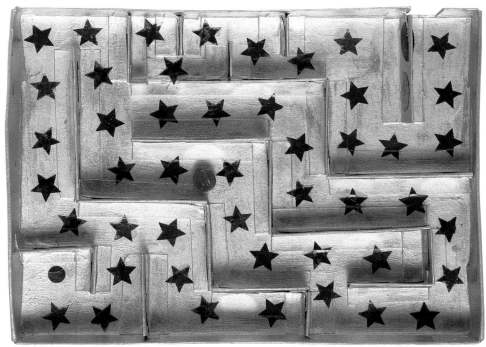

Roll your marble through the maze to the red spot

1 Draw the outline of a maze in your box lid and make a narrow opening at the start point.

2 Cut strips of card for the maze walls. Fold along the dotted lines.

3 Glue the strips along the pencil lines.

4 When dry, paint the whole maze silver.

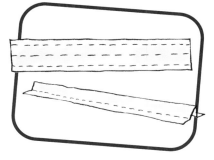

5 Decorate the maze walls with cut up sequins.

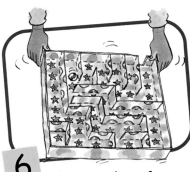

6 Now see how fast you can get the marble through the maze!

23

Paper homes

Wasps belong to a large group of insects called Hymenoptera. Although some kinds of wasps live on their own, most live in large social groups known as colonies.

Usually the colony has a queen. Only the queen wasp will mate and produce eggs. The other females are workers, while male wasps only visit to mate with the queen.

PULP AND PAPER

The queen chooses the nesting place, which must be warm and dry. She uses her strong jaws to tear wood from twigs, fences or even wooden beams. Then she chews the wood into a soft pulp. This turns into a kind of paper when it dries, and is used to build the nest. The queen builds the first cells or comb. These are safe places where the young wasps will grow. When the first comb of five to ten cells is built, she lays one egg in each cell and glues it to the inside.

SILKEN COCOONS

Twenty days later the young wasps fill their cells and begin to build a cocoon of silk thread. The queen builds a protective wall called an envelope around the cocoons. After another twenty days the wasps hatch. All of them are female. They help the queen to build more cells.

MULTI-STOREY COMBS

The female workers construct a new comb by joining it to the first with a pillar. As more wasps are born, more combs and pillars are made, and the nest grows bigger. The very last cells to be made are bigger than the rest. They contain male wasps as well as other females that will become queens. These wasps leave the nest and mate. The males then die. The old queen and her workers stay with the nest until they die in the autumn.

Minibeasts

Queen wasp's nest

WHAT YOU NEED

egg cartons

paints

wire

tissue paper

glue

paste

cotton wool

pipe cleaners

scissors

balloon

newspaper

1 Cut out the cups from the egg cartons and paint them pale yellow.

2 Stick the cups together in a honeycomb grid.

3 Stuff some of the cups with cotton wool.

4 Blow up the balloon into a small oval and paste on three layers of newspaper. When dry, pop the balloon.

5 Scrunch up a piece of tissue paper and glue it to the end for the head. Paint on yellow and black stripes and black eyes.

Stick pipe cleaners into the body for legs and into the head for antennae. Make wire wings. Stick them through the sides of the wasp's body.

Put the queen on the honeycomb, then add some smaller worker wasps

25

Wiggly worms

Soft, squidgy earthworms soon dry up in the hot sun. That is why they live in the damp soil. They burrow through it, eating it as they go along, taking in nutrients. When the leftover soil comes out of the worm's rear end, it leaves a muddy squiggle behind, called a worm cast. Earthworm tunnels let air and water into the soil, mix up the layers and make old leaves rot away. This keeps the soil fertile and plants healthy.

WORM WRIGGLE

A worm's long body is made of many parts joined together, called segments. Its mouth is a hole at the pointed front end. A worm does not have legs, but it does have tiny hairs growing along its body. These hairs grip the sides of a worm's tunnel as it wriggles from side to side, squeezing through the soil.

WORMS IN DANGER!

Although worms have no ears or proper eyes, the front end can tell whether it is light or dark. The worm's body can also detect, or feel, very tiny movements. For example, it can feel a bird hopping on the ground above, or a mole digging in the soil nearby. It will then tunnel deeper to get out of the way. If the worm's rear end is pecked or bitten, it grows again. But if the front end is damaged, the worm dies.

PARASITES

Some kinds of worms are parasites. They live inside other animals, and sometimes also inside people. A tapeworm lives inside the gut or intestine of a larger animal, feeding on the soupy, digested food around it. Roundworms live in the stomach, muscles, intestines and even in the eyes of other animals.

A friend to gardeners, the earthworm helps keep soil fertile.

Stripey felt worm

WHAT YOU NEED

tissue paper

needle

thread

sequins

glue

felt

beads

newspaper

scissors

1 Cut different-coloured felt materials into long rectangles and 2 round-edged pieces for the head and tail.

2 Sew together with thread using a simple over stitch. Leave a small hole ready to put the stuffing in.

3 Sew or glue coloured sequins on the body.

Cut up lots of thin strips of tissue paper for a wormy bed

4 Sew on beads for the eyes and stitch a smiley mouth.

5 Stuff your worm with scrunched up newspaper or tissue. Sew up the hole to finish the worm.

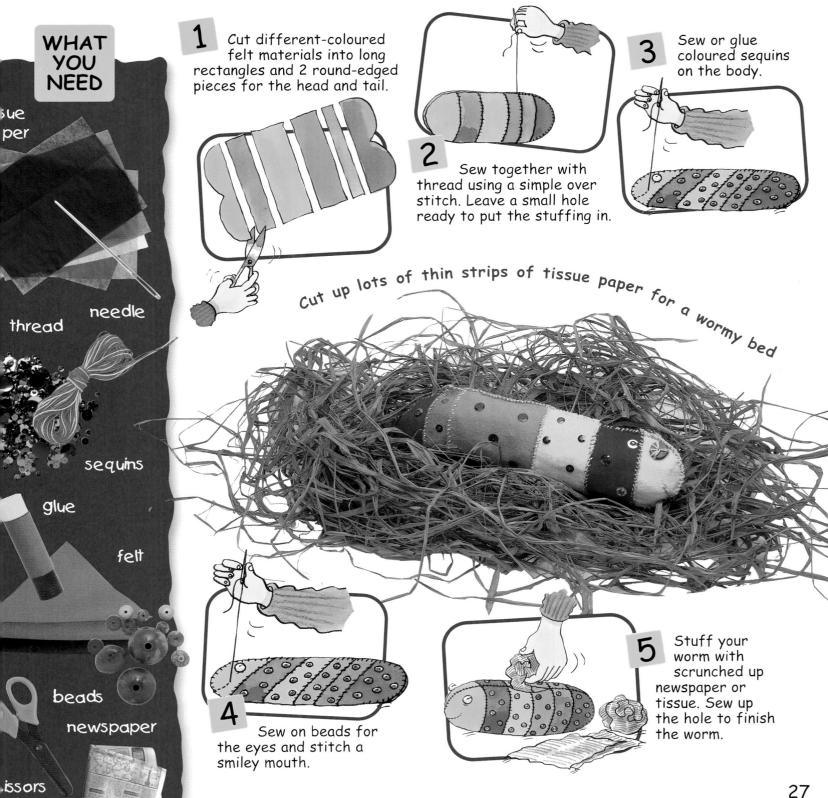

27

Magnificent moths

Have you ever watched moths flit around a light at night? They are the nocturnal, or night-time, relatives of butterflies. In fact, moths and butterflies are so alike that it can sometimes be difficult to tell them apart.

GROWING UP

Like butterflies, moths change their body shape as they grow up. They start life as an egg, which hatches into a caterpillar. The caterpillar then turns into an unmoving pupa from which, in a few weeks, a fully grown moth crawls out.

BUTTERFLY OR MOTH?

The main difference between moths and butterflies is that moths fly at night and butterflies feed in the daytime.

A bull's-eye moth displaying eye spots on its wings.

Another way of telling moths and butterflies apart is to see how they hold their wings when resting. Moths rest with their wings out flat, while butterflies hold their wings upright.

CAMOUFLAGE

Most moths are less colourful than butterflies, to blend in better with their surroundings. Many have bark or leaf-like patterns on their wings. These help to camouflage, or disguise them, while resting in a tree. Some moths have brightly coloured wings, which are just as beautiful as a butterfly's. But these moths are usually poisonous or bad-tasting! Others frighten away predators because they have large spots on their wings which look like eyes.

FRIEND OR PEST?

Moths pollinate many flowers. When they feed on a flower's nectar, pollen sticks to the moth's furry body and rubs off on to other flowers it visits. The caterpillars of silkworm moths produce silk thread which they weave into a case, called a cocoon, to protect the pupa. The thread is unwound and spun into valuable silk fabric. However, the hungry caterpillars of many moths are serious pests. They can munch their way through important food crops, or even woollen clothes, leaving annoying holes behind.

Minibeasts

Velvet moth

Put your hand inside the glove and flap the wings of your moth

WHAT YOU NEED

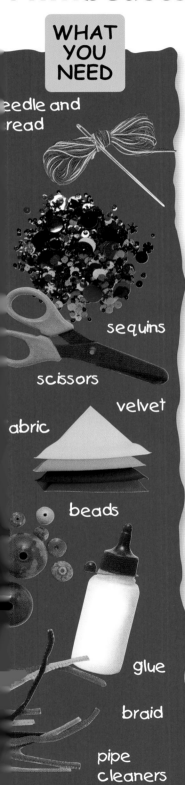

needle and thread

sequins

scissors

velvet

fabric

beads

glue

braid

pipe cleaners

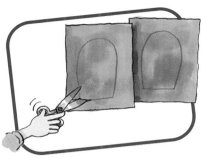

1 Cut out 2 hand-sized pieces of fabric for the moth's body, as shown.

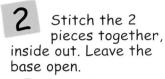

2 Stitch the 2 pieces together, inside out. Leave the base open.

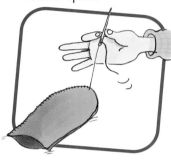

3 Cut wings and central body flaps out of velvet and fabric. Decorate with patches and sequins.

4 Turn the body the right way out and stitch on the wings. Glue the pipe cleaners on the head for antennae.

5 Sew 2 beads on to the face for the eyes. Add braid.

You can use different materials to make stripey, checked, or patchwork moths.

Jewelled webs

SILK SPINNERS

Spiders produce silk from special glands inside their abdomen. The glands make the liquid silk, which is then squeezed out through six spinnerets at the tip of the abdomen. Each spinner squirts out the silk in long, sticky threads.

A PRETTY TRAP

The large, circular orb web is the biggest and most complicated web shape. It takes about an hour for the orb web spider to spin its web. It usually does this at night or just before dawn. First, the spider makes the frame, stretching strands of silk between trees or flower stems. Then strands of silk are stretched from the centre, like the spokes of a wheel. Finally, the spider weaves the silk in between each spoke in a spiral shape. The insect trap is complete!

WEB WONDERS

Not all webs are the same. Funnel-web spiders spin a silk tube that ends in a flat sheet. The spider hides in the bottom of the tube. When an insect lands on the sheet, the spider rushes out and stabs it through the silk, then drags it down to its lair. Scaffold-web spiders spin the simplest webs. These are usually just a tangle of silky threads fixed to one point, such as the corner of a ceiling. The web-casting spider goes fishing for its prey! It spins a web between its back legs and throws it over passing flies like a net.

Have you ever watched a spider making a web? Or seen a small insect struggling to escape from its sticky strands? Spiders are master spinners and weavers who spin silk threads to catch insects for food. But only spiders with poor eyesight need webs to catch their prey.

Dreamcatcher mobile

WHAT YOU NEED

wire

beads

old thread

sequins

tissue paper

paper spider

1 Make a wire circle and wrap with twisted tissue paper.

2 Attach gold thread to the inside of the circle as shown, threading beads as you go. Finish with a bead knotted in the middle.

3 Tie dangly thread with beads and sequins to the bottom. Tie a length of thread to the top to hang your dreamcatcher from the ceiling.

Hang a friendly paper spider from the beaded web

Shield bugs

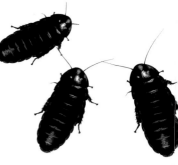

Surviving in nature is like surviving a battle, which is why many minibeasts have hard, thick covers over their bodies. This armour protects them from enemies such as pecking birds and also from bad weather, falling twigs and other dangers.

TOUGH PEST
One of the toughest bugs is the cockroach. Different kinds live almost everywhere in the world. The cockroach's flat body is protected with a tough covering like stiff leather. Long, strong legs help the cockroach to race or climb away from danger. Some types can also fly. Cockroaches breed fast, too, which keeps up their numbers. And they eat almost anything – from leftover food to the droppings of other pests such as rats and mice.

SHIELD-SHAPED
A shieldbug's hard, flat body is shaped just like the shield of a medieval knight. The green shieldbug is the same colour as the leaves it lives on, so enemies cannot see it easily.

STRONG WINGS
Like most other insects, beetles have four wings. The first two are tough, dome-shaped cases which are curved and very strong. Together, these wings cover most of the beetle's body. They also protect the thin, delicate second wings which are folded underneath.

ARMOUR PLATES
Another armour-plated minibeast is the woodlouse. Its body has about twelve wide, curved plates that look like strips of armour.

Minibeasts

Robot beetle

WHAT YOU NEED

- see-through plastic pot
- sequins
- scissors
- glue
- polyboard
- wire
- card
- silver paint and brush
- glitter
- pipe cleaners
- wooden sticks

1 Draw the shapes on card as shown and cut out.

2 Paint both cut-out shapes silver and glue glitter to the long strip.

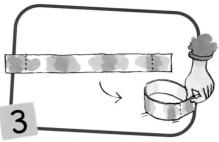

3 Make folds in the long piece as shown and glue ends together.

4 Decorate the rounded cut-out with sequins, wire and glitter. Glue onto the base.

5 Cut out 6 wheels from the polyboard and paint or colour.

6 Poke the 3 sticks through the base and push on the wheels.

Glue on the plastic top. Add sequins for eyes and pipe-cleaner antennae.

Design and make all kinds of armour-plated robot minibeasts

Hoppers and hunters

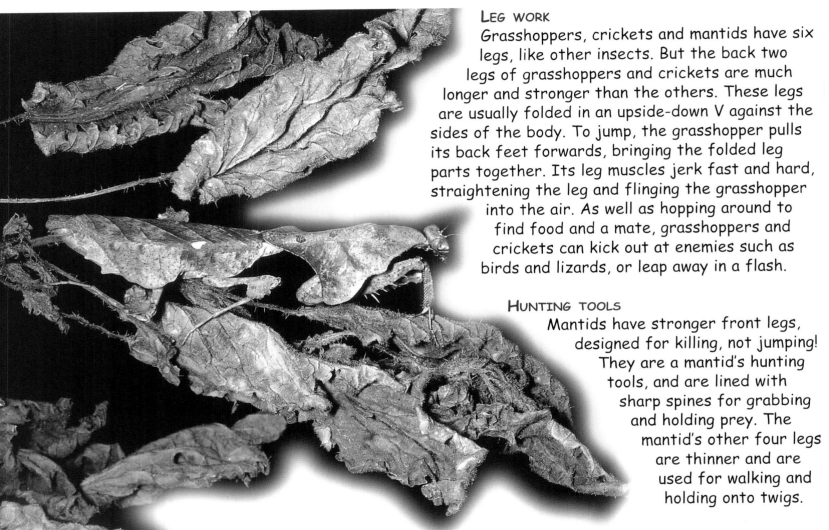

LEG WORK

Grasshoppers, crickets and mantids have six legs, like other insects. But the back two legs of grasshoppers and crickets are much longer and stronger than the others. These legs are usually folded in an upside-down V against the sides of the body. To jump, the grasshopper pulls its back feet forwards, bringing the folded leg parts together. Its leg muscles jerk fast and hard, straightening the leg and flinging the grasshopper into the air. As well as hopping around to find food and a mate, grasshoppers and crickets can kick out at enemies such as birds and lizards, or leap away in a flash.

HUNTING TOOLS

Mantids have stronger front legs, designed for killing, not jumping! They are a mantid's hunting tools, and are lined with sharp spines for grabbing and holding prey. The mantid's other four legs are thinner and are used for walking and holding onto twigs.

Which insects put their legs to powerful use? Grasshoppers and crickets are the champion hoppers of the insect world. They can leap about 200 times their own length! Mantids, one of the fiercest predators of the insect world, use their strong front legs to strike out with lightning-fast speed at their prey.

CHIRP-CHIRP

Quickly rub your fingernail across the teeth of a plastic comb – "zip-zip-zip"! On a warm summer's day, you can hear a similar sound coming from grass and bushes. It's male grasshoppers and crickets 'singing' to attract females of their kind for breeding. Most grasshoppers sing by rubbing a hard ridge on their flap-like front wings along a row of tiny knobs on their back legs. Crickets rub together the spiky veins on their two front wings.

Grinning grasshoppers

Make bouncing green grasshoppers with funny faces

WHAT YOU NEED

- wire
- sequins
- glue
- tissue paper
- polyboard
- paper
- tape
- scissors
- crayons
- pipe cleaners

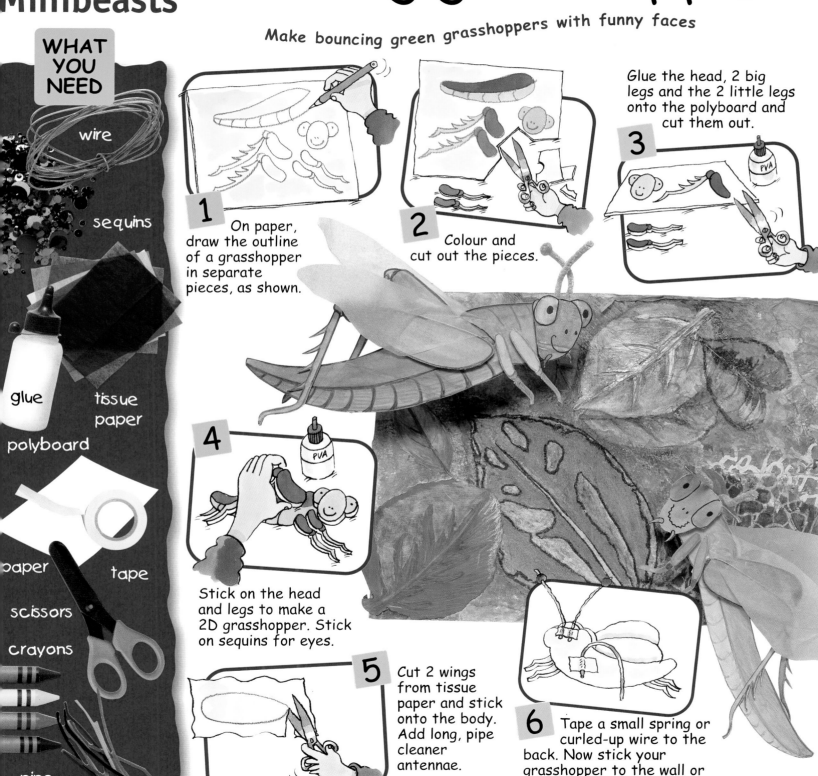

1 On paper, draw the outline of a grasshopper in separate pieces, as shown.

2 Colour and cut out the pieces.

Glue the head, 2 big legs and the 2 little legs onto the polyboard and cut them out.
3

4 Stick on the head and legs to make a 2D grasshopper. Stick on sequins for eyes.

5 Cut 2 wings from tissue paper and stick onto the body. Add long, pipe cleaner antennae.

6 Tape a small spring or curled-up wire to the back. Now stick your grasshopper to the wall or ceiling and watch it bounce!

Stick thin

CAMOUFLAGE CHAMPIONS

Stick insects are also called walking sticks, phasmids, spectre or ghost insects. Their long, thin bodies and legs are usually coloured green or brown, and they look exactly like sticks or twigs. Enemies, such as birds, do not notice them because they are so well camouflaged. Not only are they shaped and coloured to look like twigs or stems, but their bodies also have small ridges, lumps, bumps or spikes, just like the bark and twigs all around them.

RAINING EGGS

At breeding time, each female stick insect lays her eggs by letting them fall to the ground, one by one. If many stick insects are laying, the falling eggs sound like the patter of rain. The eggs look like plant seeds, and usually hatch after a year. Then the tiny youngsters, called nymphs, crawl up the nearest tree and begin munching leaves.

The stick insect really looks like its name! Can you tell where it is?

At sunset in a tropical forest, many animals settle down to sleep. But this is also the time when lots of other creatures wake up to feed. In the daytime, stick insects stay quite still, hidden in bushes and trees. When they wake up at night, they move about very slowly, feeding on leaves and buds. There are so many, it looks as if hundreds of twigs and stems have come alive!

FIGHTING BACK

A bird, lizard or other attacking predator may get a surprise. The stick insect might fold up its legs and fall to the ground or open its large, bright rear wings to show a sudden flash of colour. It might also throw up smelly, half-digested food, kick with its spiky legs, or squirt out foul, stinging liquid.

Minibeasts

Stick insect parade

WHAT YOU NEED

pipe cleaners

glue

...sh

green paint

sequins

...all plant

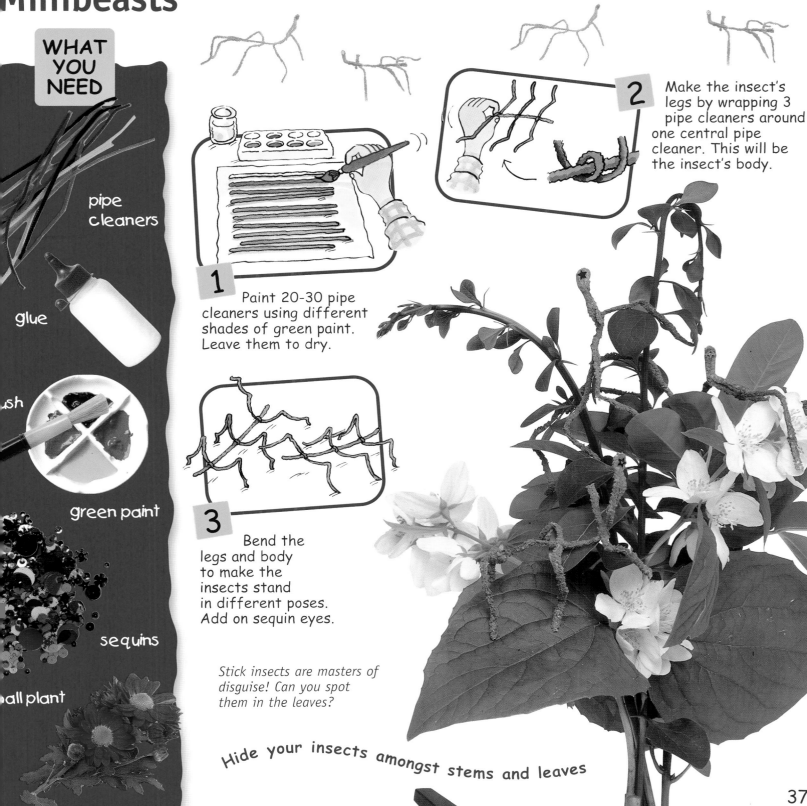

1 Paint 20-30 pipe cleaners using different shades of green paint. Leave them to dry.

2 Make the insect's legs by wrapping 3 pipe cleaners around one central pipe cleaner. This will be the insect's body.

3 Bend the legs and body to make the insects stand in different poses. Add on sequin eyes.

Stick insects are masters of disguise! Can you spot them in the leaves?

Hide your insects amongst stems and leaves

Wood whittlers

The young, or larvae, of wood-boring beetles are expert wood carvers. They spend their time chewing through wood, making tunnels as they eat. Throughout its life cycle, a beetle changes shape four times, in a process called metamorphosis. It is born as an egg, and hatches into a larva before becoming a pupa. Finally, a fully-grown adult beetle emerges.

HUNGRY BURROWERS

Wood-boring beetles such as deathwatch and bark beetles, lay their eggs just under the bark of trees, or other kinds of wood. When the eggs hatch, the larvae burrow down into the wood where they are surrounded by food, and are safe from hungry predators. They stay here until they become fully-grown beetles. Most adult beetles then crawl out and start feeding on a different type of food, such as flower pollen. Some carry on eating wood as adults.

DRILLING AND BORING

Beetle larvae use their chewing mouthparts to drill tunnels in front of them. If there are beetle larvae in bark or wood, you can see the tiny sawdust trails coming out from the tunnels that they have bored. You can also see the holes left by the fully-grown beetles when they leave their woody homes.

LITTLE PESTS

Many wood-boring beetles or their larvae are pests, causing serious damage to buildings, furniture or trees. The larvae of the elm bark beetle spread Dutch elm disease, which kills elm trees by carrying a fungus from tree to tree. In houses, the deathwatch beetle can turn timber beams into skeletons. It prefers wood that is over a hundred years old, and many historic buildings have been ruined by this hungry beetle's tunnelling.

A close-up of the tunnels left by wood-boring beetles under tree bark.

Woodsculpture

Minibeasts

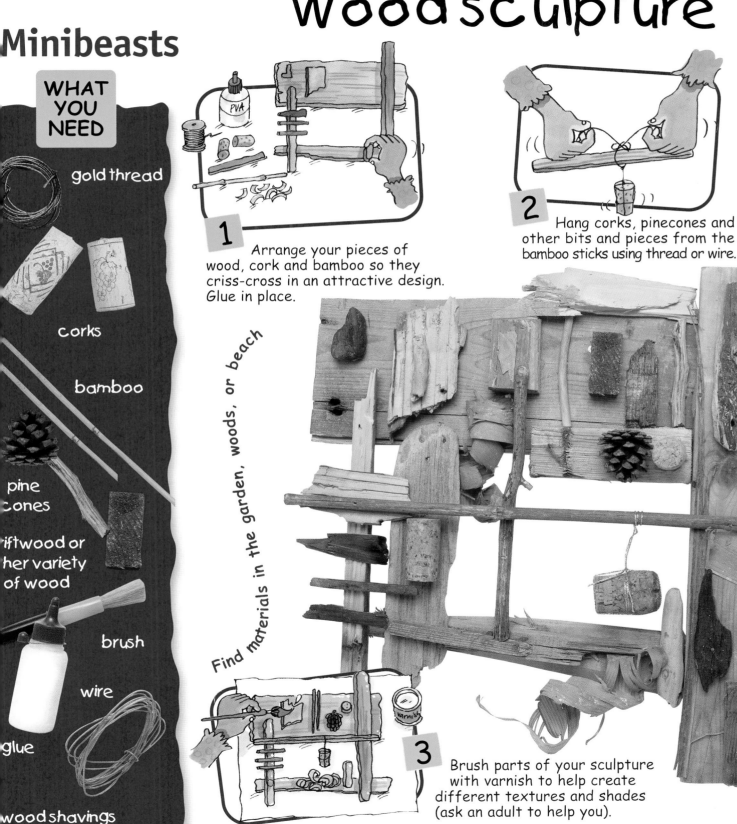

WHAT YOU NEED

gold thread

corks

bamboo

pine cones

driftwood or other variety of wood

brush

wire

glue

wood shavings

varnish

1 Arrange your pieces of wood, cork and bamboo so they criss-cross in an attractive design. Glue in place.

2 Hang corks, pinecones and other bits and pieces from the bamboo sticks using thread or wire.

Find materials in the garden, woods, or beach

3 Brush parts of your sculpture with varnish to help create different textures and shades (ask an adult to help you).

Termite towers

Imagine a gigantic skyscraper with a busy city inside it. There are hundreds of rooms, corridors, food stores, a huge nursery and an air-conditioning system! It is an amazing termite tower!

SKY HIGH

Termites live in groups called colonies in hot, dry parts of the world. They protect their nest by building a tower on top of it, which is sometimes more than six metres tall. If termites were the same size as people, their towers would be six times higher than the world's tallest skyscrapers!

SOIL CITY

Termites usually make the tower from soil, chewing and moistening it into shape. When the soil dries it is as hard as brick. Inside the tower, tubes called chimneys let air flow up from the underground nest, keeping it cool and damp. The tower not only protects the termites from drying out in the sun, but also from many enemies, including ants, lizards, birds and ant-eaters.

BUSY WORKERS

Termites are blind and live underground nearly all their lives. Termite workers have different jobs. Some gather food, some guard the nest, while others carry away rubbish or repair the tower. Babysitter workers have the important task of looking after the eggs, which are laid only by the bigger queen termite. For about five years, the queen lays twenty eggs every minute. As soon as an egg hatches, the young termite begins work.

Minibeasts

Junk tower

Make termite models for your tower!

WHAT YOU NEED

card tubes

paste

newspaper

ck ard

sue per

paint

glue

ottletops

straws

lids

plastic spoons

1 Stick a length of cardboard tube to a square piece of card.

2 Scrunch up newspaper and glue around the tube, building up the shape of a termite tower.

3 Paste on layers of tissue paper.

4 Glue junk, such as bottletops, straws, plastic spoons, or wooden sticks, onto your tower.

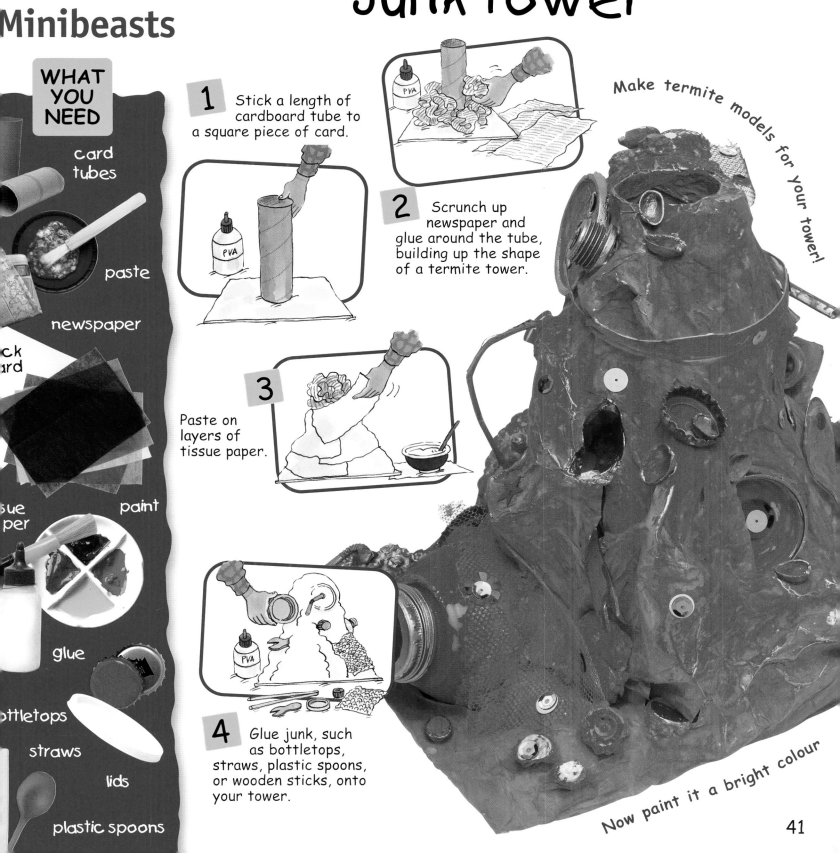

Now paint it a bright colour

Rowers and skaters

Do you wish you could run on water, or swim as fast as a speedboat? Some insects can! Pondskaters scoot across the surface of water, while backswimmers and water-boatmen row along at amazing speeds.

STAYING ON TOP
The pondskater is a very small, light insect. This fact, and the brush-like hairs on the undersides of its feet that trap tiny bubbles of air, help it to stay afloat. To skate across the water, it uses its long middle legs like a pair of oars and steers with its back legs. Pondskaters can feel the ripples sent out across the water's surface by a struggling insect. These tell the pondskater which way to skid and slide to find its meal.

UPSIDE-DOWN HUNTER
The backswimmer hangs just underneath the water's surface. Like the pondskater, the backswimmer feels the ripples made by struggling prey. It rows over at top speed, jerking its big rear legs forwards and backwards like oars.

ON THE BOTTOM
A water-boatman looks similar to a backswimmer, but it lives the right way up on the bottom of the pond. It rows through the water using its paddle-shaped back legs, clings to weeds with its middle legs, and scoops up plants with its front legs.

Minibeasts

WHAT YOU NEED

large plastic bottle

glue

masking tape

scissors

acrylic paint and brush

sequins

corrugated card

8 wooden sticks

foil

Rowing boat

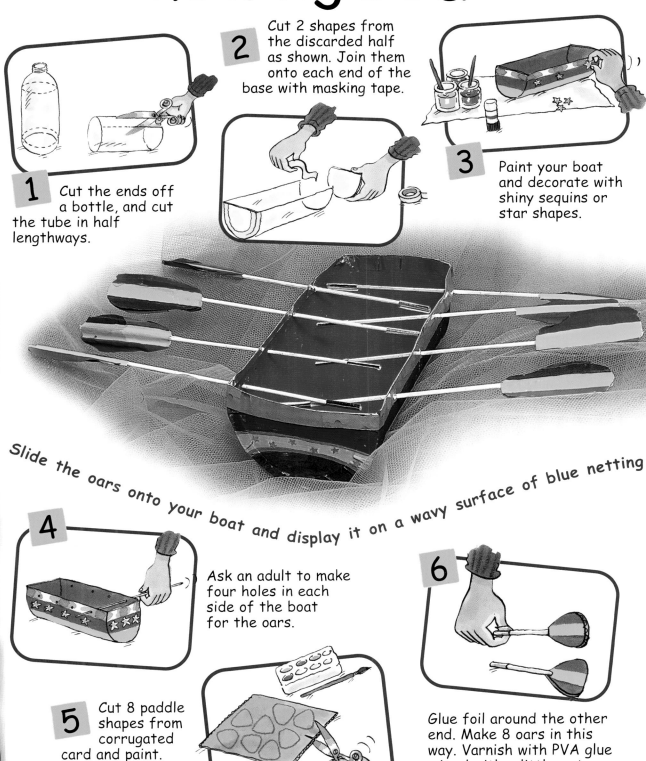

1 Cut the ends off a bottle, and cut the tube in half lengthways.

2 Cut 2 shapes from the discarded half as shown. Join them onto each end of the base with masking tape.

3 Paint your boat and decorate with shiny sequins or star shapes.

Slide the oars onto your boat and display it on a wavy surface of blue netting

4 Ask an adult to make four holes in each side of the boat for the oars.

5 Cut 8 paddle shapes from corrugated card and paint. Glue a paddle to one end of each stick.

6 Glue foil around the other end. Make 8 oars in this way. Varnish with PVA glue mixed with a little water.

Nightlights

The glowing light trail left by a flashing firefly.

On a warm, clear summer's evening, just as it is beginning to get dark, you might see a small, bright light dart suddenly across the sky – it is a firefly! Fireflies are a kind of small beetle, whose bodies glow with a yellowish light. The light is made by a special substance, called luciferin, in the firefly's skin.

COLD GLOW

When an electric light bulb shines, it gets hot. But a firefly's glow is a cold light, like that of most creatures which make their own 'living light'. The flashlight fish is the brightest light-maker. Its light can be seen from thirty metres away.

FLASHING CODES

Fireflies glow in the dark to find a mate. The males flit about, flashing their lights on and off. The females sit on nearby twigs and bushes, and flash their own lights in reply. Each species of firefly has its own code of flashes. This way, the males and females recognise their own kind and can get together to breed.

GLOWING WORM

The glow-worm is another kind of beetle that shines in the dark. In the evening, the wingless female crawls up a stem or twig, and twists herself around to show the light shining from her rear underside. Male glow-worms have no light. They fly about, looking for the shining females so they can breed.

Minibeasts

WHAT YOU NEED

black card

silver and gold paint

tissue paper

brush

glue

gold thread

glitter

wire

tape

sequins

1 Decorate a piece of black card with glitter, sequins and metallic paints.

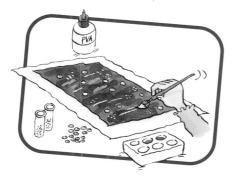

2 Scrunch the tissue paper into round body shapes and into tiny round balls for eyes.

3 Make wire wing shapes and cover with tissue paper.

4 Fix the wings around the tissue paper bodies. Stick on the tiny tissue paper eyes.

5

Hang glittery, glowing fireflies against a night sky

Spread glue over the bodies and dip them into glitter.

Tie gold thread around each firefly. Hang in front of your nightlight background, taping the threads onto the back.

45

Glossary and Index

abdomen The rear section of an insect's body. 10, 30, 42

ant 22, 40

ant-eater 40

antennae (singular: antenna) A pair of sensitive structures on an insect's head. Insects sense things about their surroundings by smell, taste and touch, and their antennae help them do this. 10

aphids Small insects that feed by sucking the juices from plants. 4

bee 6

beetle 4, 16, 32, 38

breed To produce babies. 44

butterfly 10, 14, 16, 28

camouflage The patterns or colours on an animal's skin that allow it to hide without being seen. 28, 36

cannibal An animal that eats members of its own species. 18, 20

carnivore A meat-eating animal. 18, 20

caterpillar 10

centipede 18

cockroach 32

cocoon A case made of silken threads that protects the pupae of insects such as butterflies. 24

colony A group of the same type of animals or plants that live or grow together. 6, 22, 24, 40

combs The regular-shaped chambers that make up the nest of wasps and bees. 24

compound eye An eye that is made up of hundreds of different parts, called facets. Each facet has a tiny lens on its surface 16

cricket 34

deathwatch beetle 38

disguise To change the appearance in order to look like something else or to hide.

dragonfly 8

drone A male bee whose only job is to mate with the queen bee. 6

earthworm 26

egg 6, 8, 22, 24, 28, 36, 38, 40

exoskeleton The tough outer casing of an arthropod's body. The exoskeleton protects the body parts under it.

facet The tiny parts of a fly's eye which is able to detect the movement of light. 16

fang 18

firefly 44

flea 20

fly 16, 20

funnel-web spider 30

gill 8

gland A part of the body that produces special substances, such as venom or wax. 6, 30, 42

gnat 20

grasshopper 34

grub A term used to describe the larvae of many insects, especially beetles. 22

hatch To emerge, or break out of, the egg. 8, 22, 28, 36, 38

hibernate To spend the winter asleep. This helps many small creatures survive the cold of the winter months. 4

honey 6

host An animal on or in which a parasite feeds and lives. 20

Hymenoptera The name given to a group of butterflies. 24

insect An arthropod with six legs and a body divided into three parts – head, thorax and abdomen. 4

ladybird 4

larvae (singular: larva) Young insects that are different when they become adults. 6, 10, 38

life cycle The series of body changes that happen in the life of an animal or plant. 38

lice (singular: louse) A wingless bloodsucking insect. 20

lizard 40

luciferin A substance present in the bodies of fireflies which glows with a yellowish light. 44

mantid 34

marine Found in, or relating to, the sea. 12

metamorphosis The rapidly changing growth stages of the larvae of certain animals, into the adult form. 38

microscope An instrument that makes things appear larger. 14

midge 20

millipede 18

mimic To copy the behaviour or take on the appearance of another creature.

mollusc A soft-bodied invertebrate such as a snail. 12, 18

mosquito 20

moth 28

moult To shed, or get rid of, an old skin, hair or feathers. 8

nectar A sugary liquid produced by flowers. Bees and other insects feed on nectar, and pick up pollen, which they then take to other flowers. 6, 28

nest 40

nit The egg of a louse. 20

nocturnal Animals that are active at night, such as moths. 28

nutrient Any substance that nourishes an animal or plant. 26

nymph The larva of an insect such as a grasshopper. 8, 36

orb web 30

operculum An opening in the body of a marine snail. 12

parasite A creature, such as a flea, that lives and feeds on or inside another creature. 20, 26

pest An insect that damages crops, or injures livestock. 32, 38

poison Any substance that can cause damage or injury to the body, or even kill. 18, 28

pollen Tiny powdery grains made by the male parts of a flower. Seeds are formed when the pollen reaches the female parts of the flower. Bees and insects carry pollen between flowers, and this is called pollination. 6, 28, 38, 42

predator An animal that hunts and kills other animals for food. 4, 10, 14, 28, 34, 36, 38

prey Creatures that are hunted and eaten by other animals. 34

prolegs Pairs of soft legs on a caterpillar's body. 10

pupa The stage at which an insect larva changes into an adult insect. 28, 38

roundworm 26

royal jelly A substance made by worker bees that is fed to all young bee larvae, and fed continuously throughout the development of larvae that become queens. 6

queen bee 6

queen wasp 24

sap A liquid full of nutrients that is found in plants. 4

scale 14

shieldbug 32

slug 12

snail 12

soldier ant 22

species A particular type of plant or animal. Members of the same species can mate and produce young. 4, 44

spider 20, 30

spine 34

spinneret The tubes at the end of a spider's abdomen, through which it squeezes silk threads to make its web. 30

stick insect 36

tapeworm 26

termite 40

tick 20

wasp 24

water-boatmen 42

wax 6

web 30

woodlouse 32

worker 22, 24, 40

worm 18